CW00457124

The Ultimate Air Fryer Recipe Book

The Essential Air Fryer Recipe Book with Best 50 Tasty Recipes. The Healthy Way to Lose Weight

Ursula Mayert

Table of Contents

The information in the following pages is broadly considered a truthful and accurate account of facts and as such, any inattention, use, or misuse of the information in question by the reader will render any resulting actions solely under their purview. There are no scenarios in which the publisher or the original author of this work can be in any fashion deemed liable for any hardship or damages that may befall them after undertaking information described herein.

Additionally, the information in the following pages is intended only for informational purposes and should thus be thought of as universal. As befitting its nature, it is presented without assurance regarding its prolonged validity or interim quality. Trademarks that are mentioned are done without written consent and can in no way be considered an endorsement from the trademark holder.

Introduction

An air fryer is a relatively new kitchen appliance that has proven to be very popular among consumers. While there are many different varieties available, most air fryers share many common features. They all have heating elements that circulate hot air to cook the food. Most come with pre-programmed settings that assist users in preparing a wide variety of foods.

Air frying is a healthier style of cooking because it uses less oil than traditional deep frying methods. While it preserves the flavor and quality of the food, it reduces the amount of fat used in cooking. Air frying is a common method for "frying" foods that are primarily made with eggs and flour. These foods can be soft or crunchy to your preference by using this method.

How air fryers work

Air fryers use a blower to circulate hot air around food. The hot air heats the moisture on the food until it evaporates and creates steam. As steam builds up around the food, it creates pressure that pulls moisture from the surface of the food and pushes it away from the center, forming small bubbles. The bubbles creates a layer of air that surrounds the food and creates a crispy crust.

Choosing an air fryer

When choosing an air fryer, look for one that has good reviews for customer satisfaction. Start with the features you need, such as power, capacity size and accessories. Look for one that is easy to use. Some air fryers on the market have a built-in timer and adjustable temperature. Look for one with a funnel to catch grease, a basket that is dishwasher-safe and parts that are easy to clean.

How To Use An Air Fryer

For best results, preheat the air fryer at 400 F for 10 minutes. Preheating the air fryer allows it to reach the right temperature faster. In addition, preheating the air fryer is essential to ensure that your food won't burn.

How to cook stuff in an Air Fryer

If you don't have an air fryer yet, you can start playing with your ovens by throwing some frozen fries in there and cooking them until they are browned evenly. Depending on your oven, take a look at the temperature. You may need to increase or decrease the time.

What Foods Can You Cook In An Air Fryer?

Eggs: While you can cook eggs in an air fryer, we don't recommend it because you can't control the cooking time and temperature as precisely as with a traditional frying pan or skillet. It's much easier to get unevenly cooked eggs. You also can't toss in any sauces or seasonings and you won't get crispy, golden brown edges.

Frozen foods: Generally, frozen foods are best cooked in the conventional oven because they need to reach a certain temperature to be properly cooked. The air fryer is not capable of reaching temperatures that result in food being fully cooked.

Dehydrated Foods: Dehydrated foods require deep-frying, which is not something you can do with an air fryer. When it comes to cooking dehydrated foods, the air fryer is not the best option.

Vegetables: You can cook vegetables in an air fryer but you have to make sure that the air fryer is not set at a temperature that will burn them.

To ensure that your vegetables aren't overcooked, start the air fryer with the basket off, then toss in the veggies once the air has heated up and there are no more cold spots.

Make sure to stir the vegetables every few minutes. Cooking them in the basket is also an option, but they may stick together a little bit.

Fries: Frying fries in an air fryer is a good way to get crispy, golden-brown fries without adding lots of oil. Compared to conventional frying, air frying yields fewer calories.

To cook french fries in an air fryer, use a basket or a rack and pour in enough oil to come about halfway up the height of the fries. For best results, make sure the fries are frozen. Turn the air fryer onto 400 degrees and set it for 12 minutes. If you want them extra crispy, you can set it for 18 minutes, but they may burn a bit.

Benefits of an air fryer:

• It's one of the easiest ways to cook healthy foods. Used 4-5 times a week, it's a healthier option than frying with oil in your conventional oven or using canned foods.

• Air fryer meals are an easy way to serve tasty food that doesn't take up lots of space. Air fryers make it possible to cook three times as much food as you can in your microwave.

• Air fryers have a small footprint and you can store them away in a cabinet when not in use.

•They are versatile kitchen appliances. You can use them to cook food for lunch, dinner and snacks.

• Air fryers require little to no fussing in the kitchen. You can use them with the lid on, which means there's less washing up to do.

Marinated Duck Breasts

Intermediate Recipe

Preparation Time: 1 day

Cooking Time: 20 minutes

Servings: 2

Ingredients:

1 duck breasts

2 1 cup white wine

3 ¼ cup soy sauce

4 garlic cloves, minced

5 tarragon springs

6 Salt and black pepper to the taste

7 1 tablespoon butter

8 ¼ cup sherry wine

Directions:

- In a bowl, mix duck breasts with white wine, soy sauce, garlic, tarragon, salt and pepper, toss well and keep in the fridge for 1 day. Transfer duck breasts to your preheated air fryer at 350 degrees F and cook for 10 minutes, flipping halfway.

- Meanwhile, pour the marinade in a pan, heat up over medium heat, add butter and sherry, stir, bring to a simmer, cook for 5 minutes and take off heat. Divide duck breasts on plates, Drizzle with sauce all over and serve. Enjoy!

Nutrition:

Calories 475

Fat 12

Carbs 10

Protein 48

Chicken and Radish Mix

Basic Recipe

Preparation Time: 10 minutes

Cooking Time: 30 minutes

Servings: 4

Ingredients:

1. chicken things, bone-in
2. Salt and black pepper to the taste
3. 1 tablespoon olive oil
4. 1 cup chicken stock
5. radishes, halved
6. 1 teaspoon sugar
7. carrots cut into thin sticks
8. tablespoon chives, chopped

Directions:

- Heat up a pan that fits your air fryer over medium heat, add stock, carrots, sugar and radishes, stir gently, reduce heat to medium, cover pot partly and simmer for 20 minutes Rub chicken with olive oil, season with salt and pepper, put in your air fryer and cook at 350 degrees F for 4 minutes.
- Add chicken to radish mix, toss, introduce everything in your air fryer, cook for 4 minutes more, divide among plates and serve. Enjoy!

Nutrition:

Calories 237

Fat 10

Carbs 19

Protein 29

Chicken Breasts and BBQ Chili Sauce

Basic Recipe

Preparation Time: 10 minutes

Cooking Time: 20 minutes

Servings: 6

Ingredients:

1   cups chili sauce

2   cups ketchup

3   1 cup pear jelly

4   ¼ cup honey

5   ½ teaspoon liquid smoke

6   1 teaspoon chili powder

7   1 teaspoon mustard powder

8   1 teaspoon sweet paprika

9   Salt and black pepper to the taste

10 1 teaspoon garlic powder

11 chicken breasts, skinless and boneless

Directions:

- Season chicken breasts with salt and pepper, put in preheated air fryer and cook at 350 degrees F for 10 minutes Meanwhile, heat up a pan with the chili sauce over medium heat, add ketchup, pear jelly, honey, liquid smoke, chili powder, mustard powder, sweet paprika, salt, pepper and the garlic powder, stir, bring to a simmer and cook for 10 minutes Add air fried chicken breasts, toss well, divide among plates and serve. Enjoy!

Nutrition:

Calories 473

Fat 13

Carbs 39

Protein 33

Duck Breasts and Mango Mix

Intermediate Recipe

Preparation Time: 1 hour

Cooking Time: 20 minutes

Servings: 4

Ingredients:

1   duck breasts

2   1 and ½ tablespoons lemongrass, chopped

3   tablespoons lemon juice

4   tablespoons olive oil

5   Salt and black pepper to the taste

6   garlic cloves, minced

7   For the mango mix:

8   1 mango, peeled and chopped

9   1 tablespoon coriander, chopped

10 1 red onion, chopped

11 1 tablespoon sweet chili sauce

12 1 and ½ tablespoon lemon juice

13 1 teaspoon ginger, grated

14 ¾ teaspoon sugar

Directions:

- In a bowl, mix duck breasts with salt, pepper, lemongrass, 3 tablespoons lemon juice, olive oil and garlic, toss well, keep in the fridge for 1 hour, transfer to your air fryer and cook at 360 degrees F for 10 minutes, flipping once.

- Meanwhile, in a bowl, mix mango with coriander, onion, chili sauce, lemon juice, ginger and sugar and toss well. Divide duck on plates, add mango mix on the side and serve. Enjoy!

Nutrition:

Calories 465

Fat 11

Carbs 29

Protein 38

Quick Creamy Chicken Casserole

Basic Recipe

Preparation Time: 10 minutes

Cooking Time: 15 minutes

Servings: 4

Ingredients:

1. ounces spinach, chopped
2. tablespoons butter
3. tablespoons flour
4. 1 and ½ cups milk
5. ½ cup parmesan, grated
6. ½ cup heavy cream
7. Salt and black pepper to the taste
8. cup chicken breasts, skinless, boneless and cubed
9. 1 cup bread crumbs

Directions:

- Heat up a pan with the butter over medium heat, add flour and stir well. Add milk, heavy cream and parmesan, stir well, cook for 1-2 minutes more and take off heat. In a pan that fits your air fryer, spread chicken and spinach. Add salt and pepper and toss. Add cream mix and spread, sprinkle bread crumbs on top, introduce in your air fryer and cook at 350 for 12 minutes Divide chicken and spinach mix on plates and serve. Enjoy!

Nutrition:

Calories 321

Fat 9

Carbs 22

Protein 17

Chicken and Peaches

Basic Recipe

Preparation Time: 10 minutes

Cooking Time: 30 minutes

Servings: 6

Ingredients:

1   1 whole chicken, cut into medium pieces

2   ¾ cup water

3   1/3 cup honey

4   Salt and black pepper to the taste

5   ¼ cup olive oil

6   peaches, halved

Directions:

- Put the water in a pot, bring to a simmer over medium heat, add honey, whisk really well and leave aside. Rub chicken pieces with the oil, season with salt and pepper, place in your air fryer's basket and cook at 350 degrees F for 10 minutes Brush chicken with some of the honey mix, cook for 6 minutes more, flip again, brush one more time with the honey mix and cook for 7 minutes more. Divide chicken pieces on plates and keep warm. Brush peaches with what's left of the honey marinade, place them in your air fryer and cook them for 3 minutes Divide among plates next to chicken pieces and serve. Enjoy!

Nutrition:

Calories 430

Fat 14

Carbs 15

Protein 20

Tea Glazed Chicken

Basic Recipe

Preparation Time: 10 minutes

Cooking Time: 30 minutes

Servings: 6

Ingredients:

1. ½ cup apricot preserves
2. ½ cup pineapple preserves
3. chicken legs
4. 1 cup hot water
5. black tea bags
6. 1 tablespoon soy sauce
7. 1 onion, chopped
8. ¼ teaspoon red pepper flakes
9. 1 tablespoon olive oil
10. Salt and black pepper to the taste
11. chicken legs

Directions:

- Put the hot water in a bowl, add tea bags, leave aside covered for 10 minutes, discard bags at the end and transfer tea to another bowl. Add soy sauce, pepper flakes, apricot and pineapple preserves, whisk really well and take off heat.

- Season chicken with salt and pepper, rub with oil, put in your air fryer and cook at 350 degrees F for 5 minutes Spread onion on the bottom of a baking dish that fits your air fryer, add chicken pieces, Drizzle with the tea glaze on top, introduce in your air fryer and cook at 320 degrees F for 25 minutes Divide everything on plates and serve. Enjoy!

Nutrition:

Calories 298

Fat 14

Carbs 14

Protein 30

Ratatouille

Basic Recipe

Preparation Time: 10 minutes

Cooking Time: 20 minutes

Servings: 4

Ingredients:

1. Roma tomatoes, seeded and chopped
2. garlic cloves, sliced
3. 1 baby eggplant, peeled and chopped
4. 1 red bell pepper, chopped
5. 1 yellow bell pepper, chopped
6. 1 small onion, chopped
7. 1 teaspoon Italian seasoning
8. 1 teaspoon olive oil

Directions:

- In a medium metal bowl, gently combine the tomatoes, garlic, eggplant, red and yellow bell peppers, onion, Italian seasoning, and olive oil. Place the bowl in the air fryer. Roast for 12 to 16 minutes, stirring once, until the vegetables are tender. Serve warm or cold.

Nutrition:

Calories 69

Fat 2g

Protein 2g

Carbs 11g

Vegetable Egg Rolls

Basic Recipe

Preparation Time: 15 minutes

Cooking Time: 10 minutes

Servings: 4

Ingredients:

1. ½ cup chopped yellow summer squash
2. ⅓ cup grated carrot
3. ½ cup chopped red bell pepper
4. scallions, white and green parts, chopped
5. 1 teaspoon low-sodium soy sauce
6. egg roll wrappers (see Tip)
7. 1 tablespoon cornstarch
8. 1 egg, beaten

Directions:

- In a medium bowl, mix the yellow squash, carrot, red bell pepper, scallions, and soy sauce.
- Place the egg roll wrappers on a work surface. Top each with about 3 tablespoons of the vegetable mixture.
- In a small bowl, thoroughly mix the cornstarch and egg. Brush some egg mixture on the edges of each wrapper. Roll up the wrappers, folding over the sides so the filling is contained. Brush the egg mixture on the outside of each egg roll.

- Air-fry it for 7 to 10 minutes or until brown and crunchy then serve immediately.

Nutrition:

Calories 130

Fat 2g

Protein 6g

Carbs 23g

Grilled Cheese and Greens Sandwiches

Basic Recipe

Preparation Time: 15 minutes

Cooking Time: 10 minutes

Servings: 4

Ingredients:

1   1½ cups chopped mixed greens (kale, chard, collards; see Tip)

2   garlic cloves, thinly sliced

3   teaspoons olive oil

4   slices low-sodium low-fat Swiss cheese

5   slices low-sodium whole-wheat bread

6   Olive oil spray, for coating the sandwiches

Directions:

- In a 6-by-2-inch pan, mix the greens, garlic, and olive oil. Cook in the air fryer for 4 to 5 minutes, stirring once, until the vegetables are tender. Dry out, if necessary.

- Make 2 sandwiches, dividing half of the greens and 1 slice of Swiss cheese between 2 slices of bread. Lightly spray the outsides of the sandwiches with olive oil spray.

- Grill the sandwiches in the air fryer for 6 to 8 minutes, turning with tongs halfway through, until the bread is toasted and the cheese melts.

- Cut each sandwich in half to serve.

Nutrition:

Calories 176

Fat 6g

Protein 10g

Carbs 24g

Veggie Tuna Melts

Basic Recipe

Preparation Time: 15 minutes

Cooking Time: 10 minutes

Servings: 4

Ingredients:

1. low-sodium whole-wheat English muffins split
2. 1 (6-ounce) can chunk light low-sodium tuna, Dry outed
3. 1 cup shredded carrot
4. ⅓ cup chopped mushrooms
5. scallions, white and green parts, sliced
6. ⅓ cup nonfat Greek yogurt
7. tablespoons low-sodium stone-ground mustard

8   slices low-sodium low-fat Swiss cheese, halved

Directions:

- Place the English muffin halves in the air fryer basket. Grill for 3 to 4 minutes, or until crisp. Remove from the basket and set aside.
- In a medium bowl, thoroughly mix the tuna, carrot, mushrooms, scallions, yogurt, and mustard. Top each half of the muffins with one-fourth of the tuna mixture and a half slice of Swiss cheese.
- Grill in the air fryer for 4 to 7 minutes, or until the tuna mixture is hot and the cheese melts and starts to brown. Serve immediately.

Nutrition:

Calories 191

Fat 4g

Protein 23g

Carbs 16g

California Melts

Basic Recipe

Preparation Time: 10 minutes

Cooking Time: 5 minutes

Servings: 4

Ingredients:

1. low-sodium whole-wheat English muffins split
2. tablespoons nonfat Greek yogurt
3. fresh baby spinach leaves
4. 1 ripe tomato, cut into 4 slices
5. ½ ripe avocados, peeled, pitted, and sliced lengthwise (see Tip)
6. fresh basil leaves
7. tablespoons crumbled fat-free low-sodium feta cheese, divided

Directions:

- Put the English muffin halves into the air fryer. Toast for 2 minutes, or until light golden brown. Transfer to a work surface.
- Spread each muffin half with 1½ teaspoons of yogurt.

- Top each muffin half with 2 spinach leaves, 1 tomato slice, one-fourth of the avocado, and 2 basil leaves. Sprinkle each with 1 tablespoon of feta cheese. Toast the sandwiches in the air fryer for 3 to 4 minutes, or until the cheese softens and the sandwich is hot. Serve immediately.

Nutrition:

Calories 110

Fat 3g

Protein 8g

Carbs 13g

Vegetable Pita Sandwiches

Basic Recipe

Preparation Time: 10 minutes

Cooking Time: 20 minutes

Servings: 4

Ingredients:

1. 1 baby eggplant peeled and chopped (see Tip)
2. 1 red bell pepper, sliced
3. ½ cup diced red onion
4. ½ cup shredded carrot
5. 1 teaspoon olive oil
6. ⅓ cup low-fat Greek yogurt
7. ½ teaspoon dried tarragon

8 low-sodium whole-wheat pita breads, halved crosswise

Directions:

- In a 6-by-2-inch pan, stir together the eggplant, red bell pepper, red onion, carrot, and olive oil. Put the vegetable mixture into the air fryer basket and roast for 7 to 9 minutes, stirring once, until the vegetables are tender. Dry out if necessary.
- In a small bowl, thoroughly mix the yogurt and tarragon until well combined.
- Stir the yogurt mixture into the vegetables. Stuff one-fourth of this mixture into each pita pocket.
- Place the sandwiches in the air fryer and cook for 2 to 3 minutes, or until the bread is toasted. Serve immediately.

Nutrition:

Calories 176

Fat 4g

Protein 7g

Carbs 27g

Falafel

Basic Recipe

Preparation Time: 10 minutes

Cooking Time: 20 minutes

Servings: 4

Ingredients:

1. 1 (16-ounce) can no-salt-added chickpeas rinsed and Dry outed
2. ⅓ cup whole-wheat pastry flour
3. ⅓ cup minced red onion
4. garlic cloves, minced
5. tablespoons minced fresh cilantro
6. 1 tablespoon olive oil
7. ½ teaspoon ground cumin
8. ¼ teaspoon cayenne pepper

Directions:

- In a medium bowl, mash the chickpeas with a potato masher until mostly smooth.
- Stir in the pastry flour, red onion, garlic, cilantro, olive oil, cumin, and cayenne until well mixed. Firm the chickpea mixture into 12 balls. Air-fry the falafel balls, in batches, for 11 to 13 minutes, or until the falafel are firm and light golden brown. Serve.

Nutrition:

Calories 172

Fat 5g

Protein 7g

Carbs 25g

Stuffed Tomatoes

Basic Recipe

Preparation Time: 5 minutes

Cooking Time: 20 minutes

Servings: 4

Ingredients:

1. medium beefsteak tomatoes, rinsed and patted dry
2. 1 medium onion, chopped
3. ½ cup grated carrot
4. 1 garlic clove, minced
5. teaspoons olive oil
6. cups fresh baby spinach
7. ¼ cup crumbled low-sodium feta cheese
8. ½ teaspoon dried basil

Directions:

- Cut about ½ inch off the top of each tomato. Gently hollow them out (see Tip), leaving a wall about ½ inch thick. Dry out the tomatoes, upside down, on paper towels while you prepare the filling.
- In a 6-by-2-inch pan, mix the onion, carrot, garlic, and olive oil. Bake it for 4 to 6 minutes, or until the vegetables are crisp-tender.
- Stir in the spinach, feta cheese, and basil.

- Fill each tomato with one-fourth of the vegetable mixture. Bake the tomatoes in the air fryer basket for 12 to 14 minutes, or until hot and tender.
- Serve immediately.

Nutrition:

Calories 79

Fat 3g

Protein 3g

Carbs 9g

Loaded Mini Potatoes

Basic Recipe

Preparation Time: 5 minutes

Cooking Time: 25 minutes

Servings: 2

Ingredients:

1   24 small new potatoes, or creamer potatoes, rinsed, scrubbed, and patted dry

2   1 teaspoon olive oil

3   ½ cup low-fat Greek yogurt

4   1 tablespoon low-sodium stone-ground mustard (see Tip)

5   ½ teaspoon dried basil

6   Roma tomatoes, seeded and chopped

| 7 | scallions, white and green parts, chopped |
| 8 | tablespoons chopped fresh chives |

Directions:

- In a large bowl, toss the potatoes with the olive oil. - Transfer to the air fryer basket. Roast for 20 to 25 minutes, shaking the basket once, until the potatoes are crisp on the outside and tender within. Meanwhile, in a small bowl, stir together the yogurt, mustard, and basil.

- Place the potatoes on a serving platter and carefully smash each one slightly with the bottom of a drinking glass. Top the potatoes with the yogurt mixture. Sprinkle with the tomatoes, scallions, and chives. Serve immediately.

Nutrition:

Calories 100

Fat 2g

Protein 5g

Carbs 19g

Crustless Veggie Quiche

Basic Recipe

Preparation Time: 5 minutes

Cooking Time: 20 minutes

Servings: 3

Ingredients:

1. egg whites
2. 1 egg
3. 1 cup frozen chopped spinach, thawed and Dry outed
4. 1 red bell pepper, chopped
5. ½ cup chopped mushrooms
6. ⅓ cup minced red onion
7. 1 tablespoon low-sodium mustard
8. 1 slice low-sodium low-fat Swiss cheese, torn into small pieces
9. Nonstick cooking spray with flour, for greasing the pan

Directions:

- In a medium bowl, beat the egg whites and egg until blended.
- Stir in the spinach, red bell pepper, mushrooms, onion, and mustard.
- Mix in the Swiss cheese.
- Spray a 6-by-2-inch pan with nonstick cooking spray.
- Pour the egg mixture into the prepared pan.

- Bake it for 18 to 22 minutes, or until the egg mixture is puffed, light golden brown, and set. Cool for 5 minutes before serving.

Nutrition:

Calories 76

Fat 3g

Protein 8g

Carbs 4g

Scrambled Eggs with Broccoli and Spinach

Basic Recipe

Preparation Time: 15 minutes

Cooking Time: 20 minutes

Servings: 4

Ingredients:

1. teaspoons unsalted butter
2. 1 medium onion, chopped
3. 1 red bell pepper, chopped
4. 1 cup small broccoli florets
5. ½ teaspoon dried marjoram
6. egg whites
7. eggs
8. 1 cup fresh baby spinach

Directions:

- In a 6-by-2-inch pan in the air fryer, heat the butter for 1 minute, or until it melts.
- Add the onion, red bell pepper, broccoli, marjoram, and 1 tablespoon of water. Air-fry for 3 to 5 minutes, or until the vegetables are crisp-tender. Dry out, if necessary.
- Meanwhile, in a medium bowl, beat the egg whites and eggs until frothy.

- Add the spinach and eggs to the vegetables in the pan. Air-fry for 8 to 12 minutes, stirring three times during cooking, until the eggs are set and fluffy and reach 160°F on a meat thermometer. Serve immediately.

Nutrition:

Calories 86

Fat 3g

Protein 8g

Carbs 5g

Beans and Greens Pizza

Basic Recipe

Preparation Time: 10 minutes

Cooking Time: 20 minutes

Servings: 4

Ingredients:

1   ¾ cup whole-wheat pastry flour

2   ½ teaspoon low-sodium baking powder

3   1 tablespoon olive oil, divided

4   1 cup chopped kale

5   cups chopped fresh baby spinach

6   1 cup canned no-salt-added cannellini beans, rinsed and Dry outed (see Tip)

7   ½ teaspoon dried thyme

8   1 piece low-sodium string cheese, torn into pieces

Directions:

- In a small bowl, mix the pastry flour and baking powder until well combined.
- Add ¼ cup of water and 2 teaspoons of olive oil. Mix until a dough form.
- On a floured surface, press or roll the dough into a 7-inch round. Set aside while you cook the greens.In a 6-by-2-inch pan, mix the kale, spinach, and remaining teaspoon of the olive oil. Air-fry it for 3 to 5 minutes until the greens are wilted. Dry out well.
- Put the pizza dough into the air fryer basket. Top with the greens, cannellini beans, thyme, and string cheese. Air-fry for 11 to 14 minutes or until the crust is golden brown and the cheese is melted. Cut into quarters to serve.

Nutrition:

Calories 175

Fat 5g

Protein 9g

Carbs 24g

Grilled Chicken Mini Pizzas

Basic Recipe

Preparation Time: 15 minutes

Cooking Time: 10 minutes

Servings: 4

Ingredients:

1. low-sodium whole-wheat pita breads, split (see Tip)
2. ½ cup no-salt-added tomato sauce
3. 1 garlic clove, minced
4. ½ teaspoon dried oregano
5. 1 cooked shredded chicken breast
6. 1 cup chopped button mushrooms
7. ½ cup chopped red bell pepper
8. ½ cup shredded part skim low-sodium mozzarella cheese

Directions:

- Place the pita breads, insides up, on a work surface.
- In a small bowl, stir together the tomato sauce, garlic, and oregano. Spread about 2 tablespoons of the sauce over each pita half.
- Top each with ¼ cup of shredded chicken, ¼ cup of mushrooms, and 2 tablespoons of red bell pepper. Sprinkle with the mozzarella cheese.

- Bake the pizzas for 3 to 6 minutes, or until the cheese melts and starts to brown and the pita bread is crisp. Serve immediately.

Nutrition:

Calories 249

Fat 7g

Protein 23g

Carbs 25g

Chicken Croquettes

Basic Recipe

Preparation Time: 15 minutes

Cooking Time: 10 minutes

Servings: 4

Ingredients:

1. (5-ounce) cooked chicken breasts, finely chopped (see Tip)
2. ⅓ cup low-fat Greek yogurt
3. tablespoons minced red onion
4. celery stalks, minced
5. 1 garlic clove, minced
6. ½ teaspoon dried basil
7. egg whites, divided
8. slices low-sodium whole-wheat bread, crumbled

Directions:

- In a medium bowl, thoroughly mix the chicken, yogurt, red onion, celery, garlic, basil, and 1 egg white. Form the mixture into 8 ovals and gently press into shape.
- In a shallow bowl, beat the remaining egg white until foamy.
- Put the bread crumbs on a plate.
- Dip the chicken croquettes into the egg white and then into the bread crumbs to coat.

- Air-fry the croquettes, in batches, for 7 to 10 minutes, or until the croquettes reach an internal temperature of 160°F on a meat thermometer and their color is golden brown. Serve immediately.

Nutrition:

Calories 207

Fat 4g

Protein 32g

Carbs 8g,

Pork Chops and Yogurt Sauce

Basic Recipe

Preparation Time: 10 minutes

Cooking Time: 30 minutes

Servings: 4

Ingredients:

1. tablespoons avocado oil
2. pounds pork chops
3. 1 cup yogurt
4. garlic cloves, minced
5. 1teaspoon turmeric powder
6. Salt and black pepper to the taste

7 tablespoon oregano, chopped

Directions:

- In the air fryer's pan, mix the pork chops with the yogurt and the other ingredients, toss and cook at 400 degrees F for 30 minutes
- Divide the mix between plates and serve.

Nutrition:

Calories 301

Fat 7

Carbs 19

Protein 22

Lamb and Macadamia Nuts Mix

Basic Recipe

Preparation Time: 10 minutes

Cooking Time: 20 minutes

Servings: 4

Ingredients:

1   pounds lamb stew meat, cubed

2   tablespoons macadamia nuts, peeled

3   1 cup baby spinach

4   ½ cup beef stock

5   garlic cloves, minced

6   Salt and black pepper to the taste

7   1 tablespoon oregano, chopped

Directions:

- In the air fryer's pan, mix the lamb with the nuts and the other ingredients,
- Cook at 380 degrees F for 20 minutes,
- Divide between plates and serve.

Nutrition:

Calories 280

Fat 12

Carbs 20

Protein 19

Beef, Cucumber and Eggplants

Basic Recipe

Preparation Time: 10 minutes

Cooking Time: 20 minutes

Servings: 4

Ingredients:

1. 1pound beef stew meat, cut into strips
2. 2eggplants, cubed
3. 2cucumbers, sliced
4. 2garlic cloves, minced
5. 1cup heavy cream
6. 2tablespoons olive oil
7. Salt and black pepper to the taste

Directions:

- In a baking dish that fits your air fryer, mix the beef with the eggplants and the other ingredients, toss, introduce the pan in the fryer and cook at 400 degrees F for 20 minutes
- Divide everything into bowls and serve.

Nutrition:

Calories 283

Fat 11

Carbs 22

Protein 14

Rosemary Pork and Artichokes

Basic Recipe

Preparation Time: 10 minutes

Cooking Time: 25 minutes

Servings: 4

Ingredients:

1. 1pound pork stew meat, cubed
2. 1cup canned artichoke hearts, Dry outed and halved
3. 2tablespoons olive oil
4. 2tablespoons rosemary, chopped
5. ½ teaspoon cumin, ground

---

6   ½ teaspoon nutmeg, ground

7   ½ cup sour cream

8   Salt and black pepper to the taste

Directions:

- In a pan that fits your air fryer, mix the pork with the artichokes and the other ingredients, introduce in the fryer and cook at 400 degrees F for 25 minutes
- Divide everything into bowls and serve.

Nutrition:

Calories 280

Fat 13

Carbs 22

Protein 18

Mustard Lamb Loin Chops

Basic Recipe

Preparation Time: 15 minutes

Cooking Time: 30 minutes

Servings: 4

Ingredients:

1. 4-ounceslamb loin chops
2. tablespoons Dijon mustard
3. 1 tablespoon fresh lemon juice
4. ½ teaspoon olive oil
5. 1 teaspoon dried tarragon
6. Salt and black pepper, to taste

Directions:

- Preheat the Air fryer to 390-degree F and grease an Air fryer basket.
- Mix the mustard, lemon juice, oil, tarragon, salt, and black pepper in a large bowl.
- Coat the chops generously with the mustard mixture and arrange in the Air fryer basket.
- Cook for about 15 minutes, flipping once in between and dish out to serve hot.

Nutrition:

Calories 433,

Fat 17.6g,

Carbs 0.6g,

Protein 64.1g,

Herbed Lamb Chops

Basic Recipe

Preparation Time: 10 minutes

Cooking Time: 10 minutes

Servings: 2

Ingredients:

1. 4: 4-ounceslamb chops
2. 1 tablespoon fresh lemon juice
3. 1 tablespoon olive oil
4. 1 teaspoon dried rosemary
5. 1 teaspoon dried thyme
6. 1 teaspoon dried oregano
7. ½ teaspoon ground cumin
8. ½ teaspoon ground coriander
9. Salt and black pepper, to taste

Directions:

- Preheat the Air fryer to 390-degree F and grease an Air fryer basket.
- Mix the lemon juice, oil, herbs, and spices in a large bowl.
- Coat the chops generously with the herb mixture and refrigerate to marinate for about 1 hour.
- Arrange the chops in the Air fryer basket and cook for about 7 minutes, flipping once in between.
- Dish out the lamb chops in a platter and serve hot.

Nutrition:

Calories 491

Fat 24g

Carbs 1.6g

Protein 64g

Za'atar Lamb Loin Chops

Basic Recipe

Preparation Time: 10 minutes

Cooking Time: 30 minutes

Servings: 4

Ingredients:

1. 8: 3½-ouncesbone-in lamb loin chops, trimmed
2. garlic cloves, crushed
3. 1 tablespoon fresh lemon juice
4. 1 teaspoon olive oil
5. 1 tablespoon Za'ataro

6   Salt and black pepper, to taste

Directions:

- Preheat the Air fryer to 400-degree F and grease an Air fryer basket.
- Mix the garlic, lemon juice, oil, Za'atar, salt, and black pepper in a large bowl
- Coat the chops generously with the herb mixture and arrange the chops in the Air fryer basket.
- Cook for about 15 minutes, flipping twice in between and dish out the lamb chops to serve hot.

Nutrition:

Calories 433

Fat 17.6g

Carbs 0.6g

Protein 64.1g

Pesto Coated Rack of Lamb

Basic Recipe

Preparation Time: 15 minutes

Cooking Time: 15 minutes

Servings: 4

Ingredients:

1   ½ bunch fresh mint

2   1: 1½-poundsrack of lamb

3   1 garlic clove

4   ¼ cup extra-virgin olive oil

5   ½ tablespoon honey

6   Salt and black pepper, to taste

Directions:

- Preheat the Air fryer to 200-degree F and grease an Air fryer basket.
- Put the mint, garlic, oil, honey, salt, and black pepper in a blender and pulse until smooth to make pesto.
- Coat the rack of lamb with this pesto on both sides and arrange in the Air fryer basket.
- Cook for about 15 minutes and cut the rack into individual chops to serve.

Nutrition:

Calories 406

Fat 27.7g

Carbs 2.9g

Protein 34.9g

Spiced Lamb Steaks

Basic Recipe

Preparation Time: 15 minutes

Cooking Time: 14 minutes

Servings: 3

Ingredients:

1   ½ onion, roughly chopped

2   1½ pounds boneless lamb sirloin steaks

3   garlic cloves, peeled

4   1 tablespoon fresh ginger, peeled

5   1 teaspoon garam masala

6   1 teaspoon ground fennel

7   ½ teaspoon ground cumin

8   ½ teaspoon ground cinnamon

9   ½ teaspoon cayenne pepper

10 Salt and black pepper, to taste

Directions:

- Preheat the Air fryer to 330-degree F and grease an Air fryer basket.
- Put the onion, garlic, ginger, and spices in a blender and pulse until smooth.
- Coat the lamb steaks with this mixture on both sides and refrigerate to marinate for about 24 hours.
- Arrange the lamb steaks in the Air fryer basket and cook for about 15 minutes, flipping once in between.

- Dish out the steaks in a platter and serve warm.

Nutrition:

Calories 252

Fat 16.7g

Carbs 4.2g

Protein 21.7g

Leg of Lamb with Brussels Sprout

Intermediate Recipe

Preparation Time: 20 minutes

Cooking Time: 1 hour 30 minutes

Servings: 4

Ingredients:

- 2¼ pounds leg of lamb
- 1 tablespoon fresh rosemary, minced
- 1 tablespoon fresh lemon thyme
- 1½ pounds Brussels sprouts, trimmed
- tablespoons olive oil, divided
- 1 garlic clove, minced
- Salt and ground black pepper, as required
- tablespoons honey

Directions:

Preheat the Air fryer to 300-degree F and grease an Air fryer basket.

1. Make slits in the leg of lamb with a sharp knife.
2. Mix 2 tablespoons of oil, herbs, garlic, salt, and black pepper in a bowl.
3. Coat the leg of lamb with oil mixture generously and arrange in the Air fryer basket.
4. Cook for about 75 minutes and set the Air fryer to 390-degree F.

5   Coat the Brussels sprout evenly with the remaining oil and honey and arrange them in the Air fryer basket with leg of lamb.

6   Cook for about 15 minutes and dish out to serve warm.

Nutrition:

Calories 449

Fats 19.9g

Carbs 16.6g

Protein 51.7g

Honey Mustard Cheesy Meatballs

Basic Recipe

Preparation Time: 15 minutes

Cooking Time: 15 minutes

Servings: 8

Ingredients:

- onions, chopped
- 1-pound ground beef

- tablespoons fresh basil, chopped
- tablespoons cheddar cheese, grated
- teaspoons garlic paste
- teaspoons honey
- Salt and black pepper, to taste
- teaspoons mustard

Directions:

- Preheat the Air fryer to 385₀F and grease an Air fryer basket.
- Mix all the ingredients in a bowl until well combined.
- Shape the mixture into equal-sized balls gently and arrange the meatballs in the Air fryer basket.
- Cook for about 15 minutes and dish out to serve warm.

Nutrition:

Calories 134

Fat 4.4g

Carbs 4.6g

Protein 18.2g

Spicy Lamb Kebabs

Basic Recipe

Preparation Time: 20 minutes

Cooking Time: 10 minutes

Servings: 6

Ingredients:

1. eggs, beaten
2. 1 cup pistachios, chopped
3. 1-pound ground lamb
4. tablespoons plain flour
5. tablespoons flat-leaf parsley, chopped
6. teaspoons chili flakes
7. garlic cloves, minced
8. tablespoons fresh lemon juice
9. teaspoons cumin seeds
10. 1 teaspoon fennel seeds
11. teaspoons dried mint
12. teaspoons salt
13. Olive oil
14. 1 teaspoon coriander seeds
15. 1 teaspoon freshly ground black pepper

Directions:

- Preheat the Air fryer to 355-degree F and grease an Air fryer basket.

- Mix lamb, pistachios, eggs, lemon juice, chili flakes, flour, cumin seeds, fennel seeds, coriander seeds, mint, parsley, salt and black pepper in a large bowl.
- Thread the lamb mixture onto metal skewers to form sausages and coat with olive oil.
- Place the skewers in the Air fryer basket and cook for about 8 minutes
- Dish out in a platter and serve hot.

Nutrition:

Calories 284

Fat 15.8g

Carbs 8.4g

Protein 27.9g

Simple Beef Burgers

Basic Recipe

Preparation Time: 20 minutes

Cooking Time: 10 minutes

Servings: 6

Ingredients:

1. pounds ground beef
2. cheddar cheese slices
3. dinner rolls
4. tablespoons tomato ketchup
5. Salt and black pepper, to taste

Directions:

- Preheat the Air fryer to 390-degree F and grease an Air fryer basket.
- Mix the beef, salt and black pepper in a bowl.
- Make small equal-sized patties from the beef mixture and arrange half of patties in the Air fryer basket.
- Cook for about 12 minutes and top each patty with 1 cheese slice.
- Arrange the patties between rolls and Drizzle with ketchup.
- Repeat with the remaining batch and dish out to serve hot.

Nutrition:

Calories 537

Fat 28.3g

Carbs 7.6g

Protein 60.6g

Lamb with Potatoes

Basic Recipe

Preparation Time: 20 minutes

Cooking Time: 20 minutes

Servings: 2

Ingredients:

1   ½ pound lamb meat

2   small potatoes, peeled and halved

3   ½ small onion, peeled and halved

4   ¼ cup frozen sweet potato fries

5   1 garlic clove, crushed

6   ½ tablespoon dried rosemary, crushed

7   1 teaspoon olive oil

Directions:

- Preheat the Air fryer to 355-degree F and arrange a divider in the Air fryer. Rub the lamb evenly with garlic and rosemary and place on one side of Air fryer divider.

- Cook for about 20 minutes and meanwhile, microwave the potatoes for about 4 minutes. Dish out the potatoes in a large bowl and stir in the olive oil and onions.

- Transfer into the Air fryer divider and change the side of lamb ramp.

- Cook for about 15 minutes, flipping once in between and dish out in a bowl.

Nutrition:

Calories 399

Fat 18.5g

Carbs 32.3g

Protein 24.5g

Nutmeg Beef Mix

Basic Recipe

Preparation Time: 10 minutes

Cooking Time: 30 minutes

Servings: 4

Ingredients:

1. pounds beef stew meat, cubed
2. 1 teaspoon nutmeg, ground
3. tablespoons avocado oil
4. ½ teaspoon chili powder
5. ¼ cup beef stock
6. 2tablespoons chives, chopped
7. Salt and black pepper to the taste

Directions:

- In a pan that fits your air fryer, mix the beef with the nutmeg and the other ingredients, toss, introduce the pan in the fryer and cook at 400 degrees F for 30 minutes
- Divide the mix into bowls and serve.

Nutrition:

Calories 280

Fat 12

Carbs 17

Protein 14

Oregano Daikon

Basic Recipe

Preparation Time: 10 minutes

Cooking Time: 10 minutes

Servings: 5

Ingredients:

1. 1-pound daikon
2. ½ teaspoon sage
3. 1 teaspoon salt
4. 1 tablespoon olive oil
5. 1 teaspoon dried oregano

Directions:

- Peel the daikon and cut it into cubes.
- Sprinkle the daikon cubes with sage, salt, and dried oregano.
- Mix well
- Preheat the air fryer to 360 F.
- Place the daikon cubes in the air fryer rack and Drizzle with olive oil.
- Cook the daikon for 6 minutes
- Turn the daikon and cook for 4 minutes more or until soft and golden brown.

Nutrition:

Calories 43

Fat 2.8

Carbs 3.9

Protein 1.9

Creamy Spinach

Basic Recipe

Preparation Time: 10 minutes

Cooking Time: 12 minutes

Servings: 4

Ingredients:

1. oz chive stems
2. cup spinach
3. 1 cup chicken stock
4. 1 cup heavy cream
5. 1 teaspoon salt
6. 1 teaspoon paprika
7. ½ teaspoon chili flakes
8. 1 teaspoon ground black pepper
9. ½ teaspoon minced garlic
10. oz. Parmesan, shredded

Directions:

- Preheat the air fryer to 390 F.
- Chop the spinach roughly.
- Place the spinach in the air fryer basket bowl.
- Add the chicken stock and heavy cream.
- Add salt, paprika, chili flakes, and ground black pepper.
- Add the chives and minced garlic.
- Mix gently and cook it for 10 minutes

- Blend using a hand blender. You should get the creamy texture of a soup.
- Sprinkle with the shredded cheese and cook it for 2 minutes at 400 F.
- Serve hot.

Nutrition:

Calories 187

Fat 16

Carbs 4.4

Protein 8.4

Eggplant with Grated Cheddar

Basic Recipe

Preparation Time: 15 minutes

Cooking Time: 10 minutes

Servings: 10

Ingredients:

- eggplants
- 1 teaspoon minced garlic
- 1 teaspoon olive oil
- oz. Cheddar cheese, grated
- ½ teaspoon ground black pepper

Directions:

1 Wash the eggplants carefully and slice them.

2   Rub the slices with minced garlic, salt, and ground black pepper.

3   Leave the slices for 5 minutes to marinade.

4   Preheat the air fryer to 400 F.

5   Place the eggplant circles in the air fryer rack and cook them for 6 minutes

6   Then turn them over cook for 5 minutes more.

7   Sprinkle the eggplants with the grated cheese and cook for 30 seconds.

8   Serve hot.

Nutrition:

Calories 97

Fat 6.2

Carbs 7.7

Protein 5.2

Coriander Garlic Bulbs

Basic Recipe

Preparation Time: 10 minutes

Cooking Time: 10 minutes

Servings: 18

Ingredients:

1. 1-pound garlic heads
2. tablespoons olive oil
3. 1 teaspoon dried oregano
4. 1 teaspoon dried basil
5. 1 teaspoon ground coriander
6. ¼ teaspoon ground ginger

Directions:

- Cut the ends of the garlic bulbs.
- Place each bulb on foil.
- Coat them with olive oil, dried oregano, dried basil, ground coriander, and ground ginger.
- Preheat the air fryer to 400 F.
- Wrap the garlic in foil and place in the air fryer.
- Cook for 10 minutes until soft.
- Let them cool for at least 10 minutes before serving.

Nutrition:

Calories 57

Fat 1.4

Carbs 8.2

Protein 1.3

Parmesan Sticks

Basic Recipe

Preparation Time: 10 minutes

Cooking Time: 10 minutes

Servings: 3

Ingredients:

1. oz. Parmesan
2. 1 egg
3. ½ cup heavy cream
4. tablespoons almond flour
5. ¼ teaspoon ground black pepper

Directions:

- Crack the egg in a bowl and whisk.
- Add the heavy cream and almond flour.
- Sprinkle the mixture with ground black pepper.
- Whisk carefully or use a hand mixer.
- Cut the cheese into thick short sticks
- Dip the sticks in the heavy cream mixture.
- Place the cheese sticks in freezer bags and freeze them.
- Preheat the air fryer to 400 F.
- Place the cheese sticks in the air fryer rack.
- Cook for 8 minutes

Nutrition:

Calories 389

Fat 29.5

Carbs 5.5

Protein 28.6

Creamy Snow Peas

Basic Recipe

Preparation Time: 10 minutes

Cooking Time: 5 minutes

Servings: 5

Ingredients:

1   ½ cup heavy cream

2   1 teaspoon butter

3   1 teaspoon salt

4   1 teaspoon paprika

5   1-pound snow peas

6   ¼ teaspoon nutmeg

Directions:

- Preheat the air fryer to 400 F.
- Wash the snow peas carefully and place them in the air fryer basket tray.
- Then sprinkle the snow peas with the butter, salt, paprika, nutmeg, and heavy cream.
- Cook the snow peas for 5 minutes
- When the time is over: shake the snow peas gently and transfer them to the serving plates.
- Enjoy!

Nutrition:

Calories 98

Fat 5.9

Carbs 6.9

Protein 3.5

Sesame Okra

Basic Recipe

Preparation Time: 10 minutes

Cooking Time: 4 minutes

Servings: 4

Ingredients:

1. 1 tablespoon sesame oil
2. 1 teaspoon sesame seed
3. oz. okra
4. ½ teaspoon salt
5. 1 egg

Directions:

- Wash the okra and chop it roughly.

- Crack the egg into a bowl and whisk it.
- Add the chopped okra to the whisked egg.
- Sprinkle with the sesame seeds and salt.
- Preheat the air fryer to 400 F.
- Mix the okra mixture carefully.
- Place the mixture in the air fryer basket.
- Drizzle with olive oil.
- Cook the okra for 4 minutes
- Stir and serve.

Nutrition:

Calories 81

Fat 5

Carbs 6.1

Protein 3

Fennel Oregano Wedges

Basic Recipe

Preparation Time: 15 minutes

Cooking Time: 6 minutes

Servings: 4

Ingredients:

1. 1 teaspoon stevia extract
2. ½ teaspoon fresh thyme
3. ½ teaspoon salt
4. 1 teaspoon olive oil
5. 14 oz. fennel
6. 1 teaspoon butter
7. 1 teaspoon dried oregano
8. ½ teaspoon chili flakes

Directions:

- Slice the fennel into wedges. Melt the butter. Combine the butter, olive oil, dried oregano, and chili flakes in a bowl.
- Combine well.
- Add salt, fresh thyme, and stevia extract. Whisk gently.
- Brush the fennel wedges with the mixture. Preheat the air fryer to 370 F.
- Place the fennel wedges in the air fryer rack.
- Cook the fennel wedges for 3 minutes on each side.

Nutrition:

Calories 41

Fat 1.9

Carbs 6.1

Protein 1

Parsley Kohlrabi Fritters

Basic Recipe

Preparation Time: 10 minutes

Cooking Time: 7 minutes

Servings: 4

Ingredients:

1. oz. kohlrabi
2. 1 egg
3. 1 tablespoon almond flour
4. ½ teaspoon salt
5. 1 teaspoon olive oil
6. 1 teaspoon ground black pepper
7. 1 tablespoon dried parsley
8. ¼ teaspoon chili pepper

Directions:

- Peel the kohlrabi and grate it. Combine the grated kohlrabi with salt, ground black pepper, dried parsley, and chili pepper.

- Crack the egg into the mixture and whisk it. Make medium fritters from the mixture.

- Preheat the air fryer to 380 F. Grease the air fryer basket tray with olive oil and place the fritters inside. Cook the fritters for 4 minutes Turn the fritters and cook for 3 minutes more. Allow to cool slightly before serving.

Nutrition:

Calories 66

Fat 4.7

Carbs 4.4

Protein 3.2

Chives Bamboo Shoots

Basic Recipe

Preparation Time: 10 minutes

Cooking Time: 4 minutes

Servings: 2

Ingredients:

1. oz. bamboo shoots
2. garlic cloves, sliced
3. 1 tablespoon olive oil
4. ½ teaspoon chili flakes
5. tablespoon chives
6. ½ teaspoon salt
7. tablespoons fish stock

Directions:

- Preheat the air fryer to 400 F. Cut the bamboo shoots into strips.
- Combine the sliced garlic cloves, olive oil, chili flakes, salt, and fish stock in the air fryer basket tray. Cook for 1 minute.
- Stir the mixture gently. Add the bamboo strips and chives.
- Stir the dish carefully and cook for 3 minutes more.
- Stir again before serving.

Nutrition:

Calories 100

Fat 7.6

Carbs 7

Protein 3.7

Summer Eggplant & Zucchini

Basic Recipe

Preparation Time: 15 minutes

Cooking Time: 15 minutes

Servings: 8

Ingredients:

1. 1 eggplant
2. 1 tomato
3. 1 zucchini
4. oz chive stems
5. green peppers
6. 1 teaspoon paprika
7. 1 tablespoon olive oil
8. ½ teaspoon ground nutmeg
9. ½ teaspoon ground thyme
10. 1 teaspoon salt

Directions:

- Preheat the air fryer to 390 F.
- Wash the eggplant, tomato, and zucchini carefully.
- Chop all the vegetables roughly.
- Place the chopped vegetables in the air fryer basket tray.
- Coat the vegetables with the paprika, olive oil, ground nutmeg, ground thyme, and salt.
- Stir the vegetables using two spatulas.

- Cut the green peppers into squares.
- Add the squares into the vegetable mixture. Stir gently.
- Cook for 15 minutes, stirring after 10 minutes then serve.

Nutrition:

Calories 48

Fat 2.1

Fiber 3.3

Carbs 7.4

Protein 1.4

Zucchini Hassel back

Basic Recipe

Preparation Time: 15 minutes

Cooking Time: 12 minutes

Servings: 2

Ingredients:

1. 1 zucchini
2. oz. Cheddar, sliced
3. ½ teaspoon salt
4. ½ teaspoon dried oregano
5. ½ teaspoon ground coriander
6. ½ teaspoon paprika
7. tablespoons heavy cream
8. 1 teaspoon olive oil
9. ¼ teaspoon minced garlic

Directions:

- Cut the zucchini into a Hassel back shape.
- Then fill the zucchini with the sliced cheese.
- Coat the zucchini Hassel back with salt, dried oregano, ground coriander, paprika, minced garlic, olive oil, and heavy cream.
- Preheat the air fryer to 400 F.
- Wrap the zucchini Hassel back in foil and place in the preheated air fryer.
- Cook for 12 minutes

- When the zucchini is cooked, remove it from the foil and cut into 2 pieces.

Nutrition:

Calories 215

Fat 14.9

Carbs 5.7

Protein 15.6

Butternut Squash Hash

Basic Recipe

Preparation Time: 10 minutes

Cooking Time: 14 minutes

Servings: 4

Ingredients:

1. 1 cup chicken stock
2. oz. butternut squash
3. 1 teaspoon salt
4. 1 tablespoon butter
5. 1 teaspoon dried dill
6. ¼ teaspoon paprika

Directions:

- Peel the butternut squash and chop it.
- Preheat the air fryer to 370 F.
- Pour the chicken stock into the air fryer basket tray.
- Add salt, chopped butternut squash, butter, dried dill, and paprika.
- Stir gently.
- Cook for 14 minutes
- Transfer to a bowl.
- Use a fork to mash.
- Serve immediately.

Nutrition:

Calories 61

Fat 3.3

Carbs 6.2

Protein 0.9

Butter Mushrooms with Chives

Basic Recipe

Preparation Time: 10 minutes

Cooking Time: 10 minutes

Servings: 2

Ingredients:

1. 1 cup white mushrooms
2. oz chive stems
3. 1 tablespoon butter
4. 1 teaspoon olive oil
5. 1 teaspoon dried rosemary
6. 1/3 teaspoon salt
7. ¼ teaspoon ground nutmeg

Directions:

- Preheat the air fryer to 400 F.
- Pour the olive oil and butter in the air fryer basket tray.
- Add dried rosemary, salt, and ground nutmeg.
- Stir gently.
- Dice the chives.
- Add the diced chives in the air fryer basket tray.
- Cook for 5 minutes
- Meanwhile, chop the white mushrooms.
- Add the mushrooms.
- Stir the mixture and cook it for a further 5 minutes at the same temperature.

- Stir then serve.

Nutrition:

Calories 104

Fat 8.4

Carbs 6.8

Protein 1.8

30-Day Meal Plan

Day	Breakfast	Lunch/dinner	Dessert
1	Shrimp Skillet	Spinach Rolls	Matcha Crepe Cake
2	Coconut Yogurt with Chia Seeds	Goat Cheese Fold-Overs	Pumpkin Spices Mini Pies
3	Chia Pudding	Crepe Pie	Nut Bars
4	Egg Fat Bombs	Coconut Soup	Pound Cake
5	Morning "Grits"	Fish Tacos	Tortilla Chips with Cinnamon Recipe
6	Scotch Eggs	Cobb Salad	Granola Yogurt with Berries
7	Bacon Sandwich	Cheese Soup	Berry Sorbet
8	Noatmeal	Tuna Tartare	Coconut Berry Smoothie
9	Breakfast Bake with Meat	Clam Chowder	Coconut Milk Banana Smoothie

10	Breakfast Bagel	Asian Beef Salad	Mango Pineapple Smoothie
11	Egg and Vegetable Hash	Keto Carbonara	Raspberry Green Smoothie
12	Cowboy Skillet	Cauliflower Soup with Seeds	Loaded Berries Smoothie
13	Feta Quiche	Prosciutto-Wrapped Asparagus	Papaya Banana and Kale Smoothie
14	Bacon Pancakes	Stuffed Bell Peppers	Green Orange Smoothie
15	Waffles	Stuffed Eggplants with Goat Cheese	Double Berries Smoothie
16	Chocolate Shake	Korma Curry	Energizing Protein Bars
17	Eggs in Portobello Mushroom Hats	Zucchini Bars	Sweet and Nutty Brownies
18	Matcha Fat Bombs	Mushroom Soup	Keto Macho Nachos

19	Keto Smoothie Bowl	Stuffed Portobello Mushrooms	Peanut Butter Choco Banana Gelato with Mint
20	Salmon Omelet	Lettuce Salad	Cinnamon Peaches and Yogurt
21	Hash Brown	Onion Soup	Pear Mint Honey Popsicles
22	Black's Bangin' Casserole	Asparagus Salad	Orange and Peaches Smoothie
23	Bacon Cups	Cauliflower Tabbouleh	Coconut Spiced Apple Smoothie
24	Spinach Eggs and Cheese	Beef Salpicao	Sweet and Nutty Smoothie
25	Taco Wraps	Stuffed Artichoke	Ginger Berry Smoothie
26	Coffee Donuts	Spinach Rolls	Vegetarian Friendly Smoothie
27	Egg Baked Omelet	Goat Cheese Fold-Overs	ChocNut Smoothie
28	Ranch Risotto	Crepe Pie	Coco Strawberry Smoothie

29	Scotch Eggs	Coconut Soup	Egg Spinach Berries Smoothie
30	Fried Eggs	Fish Tacos	Creamy Dessert Smoothie

Conclusion

Thanks for making it to the end of this book. An air fryer is a relatively new addition to the kitchen, and it's easy to see why people are getting excited about using it. With an air fryer, you can make crispy fries, chicken wings, chicken breasts and steaks in minutes. There are many delicious foods that you can prepare without adding oil or grease to your meal. Again make sure to read the instructions on your air fryer and follow the rules for proper usage and maintenance. Once your air fryer is in good working condition, you can really get creative and start experimenting your way to healthy food that tastes great.

That's it! Thank you!

CPSIA information can be obtained
at www.ICGtesting.com
Printed in the USA
LVHW061157160521
686961LV00036B/606/J